8 Keys To Connecting

The Communication Code of Conduct

Darren Murphy

8 Keys to Connecting

The Communication Code of Conduct

By

Darren Murphy

Nashville, Tennessee

Copyright © 2012 by Darren Murphy

Mill City Press, Inc.
212 3rd Avenue North, Suite 290
Minneapolis, MN 55401
612.455.2294
www.millcitypublishing.com

All Rights Reserved. No portion of this book may be duplicated, whether mechanically or digitally, without the express written permission of the author. Short excerpts may be used with the permission of the author for the purposes of media reviews.

First Edition: January 2012

ISBN : 978-1-937600-79-2

LCCN : 2012930433

Printed in the United States of America on acid-free paper.

Cover and interior design by Johnny King – JK Design | Graphic Communications
www.JKDesignGC.com

Illustrations by Robert Jones

For more information or additional copies, please contact:
Darren Murphy
(615) 513-2483
www.djmseminars.com
www.8keys2connecting.com or
www.8k2c.com (if you're into brevity)

→ ① Strong intros!

DEDICATION

I dedicate this book to Agnes Murphy, my mother, who believed in my ability.

Thank you, Mother, for everything.

Acknowledgments

Charlotte, my wife, deserves sainthood for: all the typing, retyping, and editing, editing and more editing. Always a teacher and forever wonderful.

Also a grateful thank-you to Angelynn Hanley and Dana Heckart for their final edits of our pre-publication printing.

Special thanks for their photo portrayals of:
Thinker - James M. Bolton
Director - Karen Grundy

Special Acknowledgment

A special Thank You to Johnny King of JK Design| Graphic Communications.

Johnny is a visual communicator by trade, and an excellent communicator interpersonally. Thank you for doing so much more than our contractual agreement. You have opened my eyes to the age of electronic communication and all the benefits therein. This book is so much better because of your skills and your understanding of both electronic and interpersonal communication.

8 Keys To Connecting

Foreword

8 Keys to Connecting is designed to be read in one to two sittings. In this format you get a complete overview of how to achieve excellence in communication. Similar to a map, you see it all in one look.

This book is the map; the accompanying web site, **www.8keys2connecting.com** or **www.8k2c.com**, takes you the rest of the way toward being an excellent communicator. It allows you to continue your journey to understanding by enabling and encouraging your commitment to learn, practice and refine communication skills and strategies.

www.8keys2connecting.com provides action plans with self evaluation measurements and video vignettes showing important communication events in the job interview. You'll also find un-solicited book reviews and recommendations, a word for the week and you and others will be able to share what you are experiencing as you begin using what you have learned in our forum. This coaching is available to help you get the skills, strategies and encouragement you need to guarantee your success as a communicator and in making Instant Connections.

Contents

Acknowledgments	viii
Foreword	xi
Introduction	xv

Chapter 1
Step Up To Real Time Communication — 1

Chapter 2
Taming Your Inner Monologue — 11

Chapter 3
Communication Impact: The Visual 55% — 23

Chapter 4
Auditory 38%: It's How you Sound — 43

Chapter 5
Content 7% : Small But Powerful — 53

Chapter 6
How People Process Information — 61

Chapter 7:
Four Personality Types — 67

Chapter 8:
The Right Impact vs the Almost Right — 77

Afterword	83
Bibliography	84
Case Studies	91
Supplemental Materials	99
About the Author	113

Introduction

There are many positives resulting from electronic communication. Students can immediately check with each other on projects or studying, corporate team members can share a multitude of materials and ideas almost instantly, international endeavors can be facilitated to a successful completion and, let's be honest, friends can just keep in touch.

It's easy, it's quick, it's relatively cheap – which taken together can produce unintended consequences.

One consequence is not being fully present wherever you are. Another is failing to attend a social occasion because it's 'just too much trouble'. And finally avoiding those social occasions because you feel uncomfortable at them.

Movies are great and I go almost weekly, but a stage play well done engages the audience in ways not found at the movie.

Books are wonderful and I love them but an accomplished storyteller who performs to a live audience creates an atmosphere rarely found in books. My wife attended the internationally famous Annual Storytelling Festival in Jonesboro, TN one year and later told me, "I feel like every emotion I ever had has been massaged."

Introduction

Whenever there are humans physically present there is the opportunity for serendipity. The potential for grasping so much more profoundly 'the human experience'.

Now here's some fantastic good news. Imagine yourself having two skill sets, electronic communication and interpersonal communication, and because of your highly developed use of these skills you become well known, referred to as the 'go to guy or gal', and you feel comfortable in both formats.

Where will you not be able to go?
    You will feel comfortable anywhere.

Who will not want to know you?
    Everyone will want to know you.

What will you not be able to accomplish?
    Nothing should elude you.

I struggle with electronic everything. It does not come easy to me. I think it has a lot to do with the mentality of the computer industry itself. When it's 80% dependable, put it on the market to sell. Well, I experienced a lot of the 20% freezes and shut downs so I began to avoid everything electronic.

I need balance. I need to learn how to use those devices. Just the other day I was intrigued while watching a colleague use their iPad to rent a car. It was quick and looked so easy. I want to be able to do that. An acquaintance who knows my struggles with technology forwarded to me a YouTube vignette called, "The Medieval Help Desk". It is so funny and so true. I identified with it totally.

This book is about sharing specific skills and strategies of face-to-face communication that when balanced with skills in electronic communication will give you the lead in all of your endeavors.

Electronic distraction ...

Take a look around the next time you're walking through the mall, dining in a restaurant, riding a bus or waiting for a class or an appointment.... Isn't it amazing just how many people are involved in some sort of electronic activity? Laptops ... cell phones ... MP3 players ... the list goes on. These things are everywhere! Even people who obviously are together in the moment are focused on these devices rather than engaged with each other. **What's up** with that? *(Just as importantly, what's the **result** of that?)*

It has been said that when Johannes Gutenberg invented the first printing press in Germany around 1450, there arose a great renaissance of thinking. As books became easier to print, they grew in numbers and spread throughout Europe and around the world! The accessibility of information and sharing of thoughts was a movement whose time had come, and the world was forever changed.

Introduction

In our generation, with the arrival of the internet and today's easy access from so many different electronic tools, the world has been forever changed — again! Only this time, the information and communications that would have taken days, weeks, months or years to travel are available in an instant. Just about anything imaginable can be found — in an instant! People can be reached across the world — in an instant! It's all very engaging, we realize.

> **However, a very real, almost shocking social problem has resulted from all this electronic "connectedness." People are becoming sadly inept at face-to-face communication!**

Think about it! A few short years ago, a group of friends meeting for dinner would enjoy spending that time together — catching up, laughing, talking over problems, sharing stories…. They'd be looking at each other and listening to each other in a healthy give-and-take. *(Those social skills, we might add here, would serve them well throughout their lives as they encountered all kinds of face-to-face situations.)*

Today, at a table for four, at least three are likely to be on their gadgets — talking, texting, typing away! The same pattern continues at home during family time … at the park/game/concert *(you name it!)* during recreational time … in the car during travel time. All this "connectedness" is resulting in an epic disconnect from—

Human interaction!

Even in this exciting digital age, interpersonal skills remain of prime importance — personally and professionally! Though it seems incredible, many have forgotten *(or simply never learned)* how to meet, greet, share, comfort and enjoy one another. Just as importantly, many have no idea how to respectfully disagree and resolve conflicts with one another.

Needless to say, there is an art to face-to-face communication, and it's not difficult to master. If you'll take the time to learn and polish the simple skills presented in this book, we believe you'll come to enjoy a level of confidence and self-assurance that will enhance all your future relationships — business and professional.

Ask yourself:

- *Do I want to make new friends?*

- *Do I want to understand others...and BE understood?*

- *Do I want to SHINE in that important job interview?*

- *Do I want to be regarded and remembered in a positive way?*

- *Do I want to experience personal and professional success?*

If your answers are a resounding YES, keep reading! What you're about to learn can to give you an edge that sets you apart from the crowd and helps you succeed beyond your wildest dreams. Prepare to dazzle your friends, your family, and more importantly — yourself!

Chapter 1

Step Up to Real Time Communication

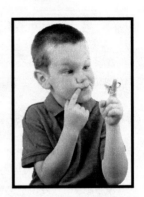

"You never get a second chance to make a first impression." — *Anonymous*

Ahh ... the anonymous life.... Whether you're shopping for clothes, researching the job market, paying bills or visiting friends, it's just so easy to take care of day to day business and communications online. "The world is your oyster," as the saying goes. You simply locate who or what you want and start clicking away. And why not? It's fast, it's easy — and when it comes to shopping, it's often less costly! We agree, it's totally cool. *(and you can do it all in your pajamas!)*

The strangest thing about it is, folks today are living their lives so anonymously *(staring into some kind of screen)* that they've forgotten *(or neglected to learn)* how to effectively communicate in person ... with real people ... real time!

This is *not* a problem your grandparents had. Then again, this book isn't written for your grandparents. It's written for *you* — today's computer-savvy, up and

Step Up To Real Time Communication

coming professional who realizes that future success *(in work and personal relationships)* is going to depend on more than techno-skills. To a large extent, it's going to depend on the quality of your —

Person-to-person interactions

There is far more to the dance of human interaction than you may think! Communication comes via body language, what one says, how one sounds — and other very specific methods! Learning how to observe, understand — and master these fascinating aspects of human nature will arm you for maximum effectiveness in just about every aspect of your life!

This book is about skill, strategy and subtlety in face-to-face communication. It is not to diminish from the fact there is skill, strategy and subtlety in cyberspace communication. These two different modes of communication have strengths and weaknesses. I propose that cyberspace communication has created another Renaissance, and in order to be an effective communicator during this Renaissance one must master both modes. To have one without the other is a self imposed handicapping of one's potential.

Here are a few strengths contained in cyberspace communication:

- *The written word can be reflected upon first providing time to organize ones thoughts and be creative.*

- *The communication interaction is recorded/ saved for later reflection or reference.*

8 Keys To Connecting

- *There is time to think before responding in a high emotion conversation*

- *One is judged/evaluated strictly on content and style of their communication, thus removing status, power and beauty from the analysis.*

Does one look 'Presidential' will not factor in, which allows for better discernment of principles, values and ideas.

First impressions

Let's say you're ordering a shirt online. Once you find the one you want, you click on the size and color, enter a credit card number, select a mailing option and click SEND. Nobody cares that you're not smiling. Nobody cares that you're in your pajamas. When you spend hours of time in situations where nobody sees you, so nobody cares — it's easy to get lazy! **Relationally lazy.** While that may often work just fine online, a bit more skill is needed in the real world.

STEP UP TO REAL TIME COMMUNICATION

Take this example:

Hal's Diner is a wireless hot spot. So, it's no surprise when Ted shuffles in with his laptop, plops it down on a table, boots up and starts scowling at the screen. He's so totally focused on his digital connection, he never even *looks up*!

Marge the waitress has seen this before. People sit in her section all the time, taking advantage of the internet and really not wanting anything *(which is fine with her, as long as they leave a tip!)* She's tempted to ask if he'd like anything, but he seems so engrossed in his laptop, she hesitates to interrupt him. *(She thinks she's doing him a favor by leaving him alone.)*

What Marge doesn't know is that Ted came in hungry. He wants a cheeseburger and fries, and he wants it now. His stomach growls. He starts to fidget. Finally, he looks up from his screen, spots Marge waiting on another table, and yells,

> "HEY! What's it take to get some service around here!?"

What's wrong with this picture? Plenty!

From the moment he walked into the diner, Ted did absolutely nothing to engage the attention of the waitress — until his outburst, that is. All it would have taken on his part was a little eye contact and a smile, and he'd be reaching for the ketchup by now! Since he totally ignored Marge and, in fact, acted as if she were not even there, Marge had no clue that he even wanted to order! She assumed by his behavior that he was only in the diner for the internet connection! Since Marge is not a mind-reader *(and Ted's body language did **not** show Marge he wanted her attention and a chance to order food,)* Ted must own his part in dropping the communication ball.

What about Marge's part in this communication failure? Does she come out smelling like a rose here? No way! Her mistake was to assume she knew Ted's intention by simply observing him. From the looks of it — even though Hal's burgers won "Best of the Best" for five years running, Ted was not in the diner to eat. So ... she neglected to ask him the one question that would have made everybody happy *(including herself come "tip time")*

"What'll ya have, hun?"

Now...we know this is a silly example. We simply use it to make a two-fold point:

1. Like Ted, we must take responsibility for clearly expressing our own intentions, and —

2. Like Marge, we must take responsibility for making sure we clearly understand the intentions of others.

To drop the responsibility ball is to regard others *(and be ourselves regarded)* as invisible. Invisible people don't get the fast service ... the good tips ... the lively friends — or the exciting jobs! Invisible people fade into the background ... blend ... settle for less than is available — just because they are *(dare we say it?)* — **relationally lazy!** *(Maybe they don't know better, but now **you** do!)*

STEP UP TO REAL TIME COMMUNICATION

> *"The meaning of your communication is the response you get back."* — *Tony Robbins*

Ted assumed Marge would come to his table, interrupt him, and take his order. But his meaning/intention as perceived by Marge was that he wanted to be left alone. (*As we've already said, Ted is responsible for having put forth such an unclear intention.*)

Marge didn't come to Ted's table because she assumed he wanted nothing more than to be left alone.

When Marge reminds Ted he never once looked up from his computer screen, so she didn't think he wanted any service, Ted might retort,

> "That's **not** what I meant!"

When Ted hammers Marge for waiting on everybody else but ignoring him, she might retort,

> "No, hun, I didn't mean it **that** way!"

Begin to Observe:

The next time you find yourself explaining, *"That's not what I **meant**."* or *"I didn't mean it like **that**."* you can be sure your intentions could have been more effectively presented! Think about what you said and how you said it *(or what you didn't say)* that was misinterpreted. Don't feel bad about it. Use it as a learning opportunity. Simply consider how you might have been more clear and direct. Next time, we just bet you will be!

Smile and the World Smiles With you

There's something extra special about **your** smile! Your smile is as unique as you are, and a smile on your face can be a great first step toward being noticed and rewarded with the service and attention you require in any given situation. Your smile is far more powerful *(and revealing!)* than you may realize, and we'll go deeper into the matter in Chapter 3. For now, keep in mind two powerful points:

> 1. **Smiling triggers the body to release the natural "feel good drugs"** — pain killers, endorphins, and serotonin. Feeling tense? Want to feel better? *(Who doesn't?)* Flash that dazzling smile!
>
> 2. **Smiling is attractive...and infectious!** You smile at someone, they smile back...and on it goes! Soon everybody feels better. According to Dan Goleman PhD., author of Social Intelligence, good feelings are more contagious than bad ones. The closer one is to depression, the more people want to steer clear. It's the positive emotions and feelings that make people want to draw closer.

So...work that smile and begin to notice what happens!

Step Up To Real Time Communication

What This Chapter Means – A True Story

I believe everyone enjoys a true story that illustrates a major point. The question was asked: Who do you remember – or who remembers you – after the important, or *(more significantly)* not-so-important transactions we all experience daily? Here is one such example which netted this lady a tidy sum.

> A few years back I was house hunting. My daughter had become interested in horses and we acquired three. It is not really possible to keep horses in the back yard of an urban home, even though it is fenced, so we began the search for a small farm located within an hour of the airport.
>
> The search became a lengthy process, more than nine months, and we were wearying. I met and dealt with many real estate agents, all of whom reminded me of trot line keepers. They didn't actively fish – they just put a line in the water with multiple hooks and periodically checked on potential catches. Then I met Larissa Lentile of Keller Williams Realty in Nashville. She had a property listed that piqued my interest. When she showed the property, she also used a sales promotion no pervious agent had used. She handed me a list of things the owners had written, identifying the reasons they loved living on that property, and this seemingly small act of true promotion netted Larissa a sales commission on a different property I did buy, using her as my agent.
>
> It also netted her a loyal customer – me – and free advertising done by me. My wife used Larissa's

insight and ability to communicate effectively when selling her house. My friends now use Larissa as their real estate representative. I have recommended her repeatedly, and it is all due to her taking her job seriously and communicating that fact to me effectively. The single most powerful skill one can have is effective communication. You can take that to the bank – figuratively and literally!

Chapter 2

Taming Your Inner Monologue

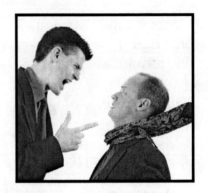

"Be the change you wish to see in the world."
— *Gandhi*

As we discovered in the last chapter, we can directly influence the outcome of a given situation based on the effectiveness *(or ineffectiveness)* of our communication. But ... how do we ensure the effectiveness of our communication? Truly, there's more to it than meets the eye!

From "barely awake" to fully conscious

Our miraculous bodies offer a number of examples of processes that go on during our waking state *(as well as while asleep)* without our conscious mindfulness. Breathing, swallowing, blinking, cell reproduction — you name it! How arduous life would be if we had to focus our minds on all these processes throughout the day.

However, another hugely important aspect of day-to-day life exists that, for most people, goes on

Taming Your Inner Monologue

automatically...without conscious mindfulness. And oh, what a trouble maker and saboteur it can be. May we introduce —

Your inner monologue

Do you ever talk to yourself? Sure you do! We all do it, whether out loud or silently in our minds. This inner monologue involves a constant stream of questions ... assumptions ... assertions.... It has been estimated that we monologue with ourselves at the rate of between 600 and 1200 words per minute! All too often, that self-talk is a loop of boring, repetitive — even faulty — chatter! Most people don't give any thought to all this self talk. Again, this is where *you* are breaking away from the pack!

Begin to notice what you're saying to yourself. What are you saying to yourself as you get out of bed in the morning ... head to class ... sit in traffic ... arrive at work? What streams through your mind as you wait for your waitress ... or walk through a grocery store? When you begin to observe yourself, you'll realize this chatter is constant! Without even thinking, there you go — yak! yak! yak!

Influencing Relationships

Our inner monologue is so important that it colors our interactions with others. It influences our relationships. Begin to pay attention to what you are saying to yourself as you encounter real time, real life people throughout your day. Pay special attention to this self-talk stream as it turns toward the significant people in your life such as your parents, friends or spouse. Really pay attention! Taking inventory of what you are saying to yourself will give you an astounding insight into the way you are experiencing others and why your relationships are the way they are — for better or worse!

If your self-talk is negative as you approach and interact with someone, that encounter or relationship is likely to be negative. Positive self-talk is more likely to produce a positive interaction, a positive relationship. In short, your inner monologue creates your perceived reality.

Since our self-talk is powerful enough to influence our interactions and relationships by creating our perceived reality, then wouldn't it make sense to *wake up* and take *conscious control* of what we're continually saying to ourselves? You bet it would! What we need now is —

Taming Your Inner Monologue

Conscious Mindfulness

How do we begin taking conscious control of important inner monologue? Simple! We do it by asking ourselves meaningful questions and sincerely wanting the answers.

Let's say, you just encountered Bob. Bob gave you a look that *did not* make you feel welcome, to say the least.

Two example inner monologue questions:

1. *Who does Bob think he is, looking at me like that?*

    This question is reactionary. You've already drawn a conclusion that Bob's actions are aggressive toward you. However, this is an unsubstantiated perception — based on observation rather than fact. Since you've already drawn this negative conclusion, your attitude turns negative. *(Can you see how this situation could quickly spiral downward?)*

2. *Is Bob mad at me...or at the situation...or both?*

    This is a sincere question. You've observed Bob's action and are wondering about his underlying intention. To be sure you understand, you are seeking more information. You have taken control of your inner monologue to accomplish more effective communication.

In this instance, your conscious inner monologue may lead you to ask for clarification. For example, you may respectfully ask...

> "Bob, I need to ask you — are you mad at me...or at the situation...or both?"

Such direct questions enable you to check on Bob's real intentions. In fact, they give him a "heads up" regarding his own inner monologue...which has affected his attitude...which has been displayed outwardly in his appearance and behavior.

Evaluate the Situation

Imagine you're a participant in one of my Communications Seminars. We've been discussing the importance of being able to evaluate situations as they unfold right in front of you. We're about to do a role play exercise. In this exercise, John is going to be on the receiving end of a tongue lashing. *(It could be from a boss, customer, teacher, etc.)*

Okay, let's role play. *(My name is Darren, and I'll play the boss.)*

>**Darren :** *(in a loud, berating tone)*
>
>> "John, everything you do is crap! I've talked to you about it repeatedly. Now WHAT are you going to do about it?"

As the recipient of this tongue-lashing, John is likely to respond in one of three typically "human" ways:

Taming Your Inner Monologue

1. He'll become a "doormat" and take the lashing.

2. He'll start manning his inner battle stations, preparing to launch a counter attack.

3. He'll become passive-aggressive, appearing to accept the verbal barrage, all the while plotting his revenge.

8 Keys To Connecting

(Were you in my seminar, it would be interesting to see how you'd respond! Typically, our participants really get into the part and start firing back at the boss! After all, nobody likes being spoken to so harshly.)

Next, we'll switch roles. John will be the boss, and I will be the recipient of the tongue lashing. *(Having just been himself berated — even in role play, John is ready to really get into the part of boss and let me have it!)*

John : *(Loud, snarling, flailing his arms....)*

"Darren, absolutely everything you do around here is total CRAP! I've talked to you about it repeatedly and I'm sick of it! Things have got to change, buddy! Now what do you intend to do about it? Hmmmm?" (The ad-libs here can be quite humorous, as you might imagine! The other seminar participants are really enjoying this.)

Before I answer, I take control of my inner monologue. I ask myself questions I honestly want to know the answer to — such as,

"Why is John yelling? What has happened? Where has he been, and who has stirred him up?"

Darren : *(Speaking calmly)*

"John, everything I do is not crap. I want to know what you are specifically talking about, and I want to fix it."

Taming Your Inner Monologue

John : *(Confused...stuttering...caught totally by surprise)*

"Uh...well...uh...."

I should tell you here that I simply *love* this exercise — not just because of the looks on all the participants' faces, but because it so beautifully illustrates the power of controlling your inner monologue!

In our follow-up discussion, the role play participant *(in this case, John)* often expresses amazement at the way I responded.

"I had no idea what to say back to you."

"Your response completely neutralized my anger. How'd you *do* that?"

To this, I usually smile and respond with ...

"I thought you'd never ask."

Six honest serving men

Regardless of the social event or situation taking place, you can take control of it and direct it by first asking six specific inner-monologue questions. These questions are key to taming your inner monologue. Rudyard Kipling called them his "six honest serving men." These simple, powerful questions are:

8 Keys To Connecting

- *Who?*
- *What?*
- *Where?*
- *When?*
- *How?*
- *Why?*

These questions are specific, and to be effective, must be asked in a sincere and thoughtful frame of mind. You must truly want the answer — the real truth. Repeat these six questions to yourself again and again until they become habit. Some habits are good, and this is one of them.

Caveat on "why?"

The question "why" is often interpreted as an objection. It may imply that you are questioning the authority of the other person to direct you. It also may imply that you are stalling in order to slow progress. *(Note how a child repeatedly asks "why" after an adult tells them to do something that they do not wish to do.)*

I strongly urge you to wait to ask "why" until much later in the conversation. Plenty of material and understanding can be gathered from "who, what, where, how and when." When this information is gathered in a neutral or positive way, the chances of the other person accepting and positively responding to a sincere "why" is greatly increased.

Remember: When asking "why," be sure to include your reason for wanting to know "why."

Example: "I want to understand why, so I can 'do/avoid/plan for' this in the future...to make it easier for you."

Who could resist such a thoughtful and cooperative attitude?

"Seek first to understand, then to be understood." — *Stephen Covey*

Best-selling author Stephen Covey thought the above statement was important enough to be Habit #5 in his acclaimed book, *The 7 Habits of Highly Effective People*. What pleases people most about others? When others truly seek to understand! What a gift it is when people really listen to us and seek to understand us by asking the right questions! What power we wield in the situation, when we offer this profound gift to others!

8 Keys To Connecting

Success Strategy:

    1. Become consciously aware of your inner monologue.

    2. Take control of it.

    3. Ask questions until it is confirmed that you understand what is being communicated.

What's the benefit of taking conscious control of your inner monologue? You attain the rare ability to control the direction of communication encounters. Think about that! By controlling your inner monologue and finding out the true intentions of another, you can greatly reduce the misunderstandings, failed relationships and regrets in your life.

You've got to admit, this stuff is HUGE! And there's more, so keep reading!

Chapter 3

Communication Impact: The Visual 55%

"When you meet a man, you judge him by his clothes; when you leave, you judge him by his heart." — **Russian Proverb**

Have you ever experienced the uneasy feeling that what you are hearing is not the full truth? Controlled studies confirm that despite what is being said, we pick up on subtle and sometimes contradictory non-verbal cues. *(We may not even consciously realize what those cues are. We just know what we're hearing doesn't quite match up with what we're feeling.)*

Let's take an example.

> Doctor A. comes into your room and remains standing in your doorway as she asks you a set of questions ... in a specific tone ... at a given delivery rate.
>
> Later, Dr. B. enters your room, smiles warmly and sits down near you. She asks you the same set of questions ... in the same tone ... at the same delivery rate.

COMMUNICATION IMPACT: THE VISUAL 55%

The *fact* is both doctors spent the same amount of time with you, but your perception is that Dr. B. spent considerably more time with you than Dr. A. In this instance, regardless of the fact, your perception is your reality.

Since perception is reality, facts must be presented so that the receiver's "reality" is what is intended. Haven't you sometimes said *(or heard,)* *"But that's not what I meant,"* or *"That wasn't my intention?"* Did you know it's a fact that what one sees has more impact than what one hears?

The 55/38/7 Percent Communication Triad

Albert Mehrabian, Ph.D., author of *Silent Messages*, established **the 55/38/7 percent communication triad**. *(Please note these three percentages add up to 100 percent.)* His background in engineering and psychology provides a unique perspective and adds to the efficacy of his research

Visual

Dr. Mehrabian discovered that what most influences or impacts the recipient of a communication is how the sender *(of the communication)* is seen. **The sender's facial expression, body position, movement and gestures all add up to the 55 percent impact on perception.** Let's call this the visual impact on the recipient's interpretation.

8 Keys To Connecting

Auditory

Next is the auditory impact at 38 percent. While not having as large an impact as the visual, at 38 percent, the auditory has a significant bearing on the recipient's perception. Is the sender's voice soft or loud? Is his cadence measured or static? Is his voice commanding ... requesting ... motivating ... debilitating? All these cues add up to 38 percent of the communication impact.

Content

The final 7 percent of communication is the content impact, the actual words spoken. Does that surprise you? Remember, these numbers give only part of the picture. Do not minimize the importance of clear content.

A master of anything understands certain parts may have more bearing or impact, but that true mastery comes from giving due diligence *(100%)* to all the details?

A master of public speaking, for example, fully attends to visual detail — from the shine on her shoes to the smile on her face. While looking great is important, he also must master the sound of his delivery. If he sounds grating, insincere, monotone or inappropriately sarcastic, then his effectiveness will lessen. Finally, though the speaker may look great and sound good, he must pay attention to each and every word he uses.

Communication Impact: The Visual 55%

Mark Twain said it best:

> *"The difference between the almost right word & the right word is really a large matter--it's the difference between the lightning bug and the lightning."*
> —*Mark Twain*

Needless to say, all three categories — visual, auditory and content — are necessary for successful communication!

Your Goal: 100% Effectiveness

In the communication game, you are competing with the unconscious patterns of your "old self." Now that you know about the 55/38/7 percent communication triad, you can pay attention to those aspects of your own communication efforts. Finally, you'll begin to get the results you want!

Mirror Mirror on the Wall

We look in the mirror all the time to check our hair, our clothes, etc. But...when's the last time you looked into your own eyes? Try it! Time yourself. Just stare into that mirror, focusing on your eyes. Does it feel uncomfortable? How many seconds can you look into your eyes before your eyes flit to your hair, your mouth, your nose — anywhere away from your eyes? Why do you think it's so difficult to stare into your own eyes?

8 Keys To Connecting

Learning to stare into your own eyes is of vital importance because it sets the stage for our learning how to control the 55 percent visual impact you present.

Here's your chance to practice how you present yourself — visually!

When you smile, do your eyes become involved, or is it just your mouth? There will be times when all you wish to convey is a social smile, performed with only the mouth. At other times, you'll wish to convey the genuine smile of heart and soul. Are there grades in between? Yes! Practice in the mirror, and become familiar with what you look like when you present each one. Practice changing the intensity of your smile. *(Just relax and have fun with it.)*

Communication Impact: The Visual 55%

Can you recall a time when you shared a specific smile, and it was received in the spirit you intended? Watch yourself in the mirror as you recreate that smile. Feel the muscles you're using. Notice the change in your eyes. Congratulations! You are learning to master conscious control of the 55 percent of visual communication impact. To perfect this conscious control, begin to observe yourself while communicating with another in…

Real Life Communication

Now go beyond observing and controlling your facial expressions to observing your body position, posture and gestures. *(Yes, the 55 percent visual involves more than your facial expression!)* What are you doing with your hands? Where is your body facing in relation to the person with whom you are communicating?

Get Conscious Regarding Your Intent!

Let's say, you're standing in an office doorway, telling someone you're glad to meet him. Maybe you have mixed wants or needs in the situation. You may want to stay, but need to go someplace else. Or … maybe you don't want to stay, but due to the other person's position of power in that situation, you must. Get off the fence and determine your intention in that moment!

Are You Congruent?

Are you partially turned away and leaning toward the door, while telling the person you're glad to meet him? Is your facial expression in tune with the rest of your appearance? Is the 55 percent visual all in line with your intent?

8 Keys To Connecting

Now ... you also need to be congruent with your 38 percent auditory category. Listen to how you're speaking. Is your tone sincere ... doubtful ... sarcastic? Is your speed and emphasis in alignment with your intention? Speed denotes your availability to the person. Tone and tempo can be aligned, but if you're zipping along *(when what is called for is a thoughtful, measured pace,)* then you are losing points from your 38 percent of auditory impact.

Are you using words that correctly explain your intent? Is your 7 percent content potential supporting your visual and auditory presentation? Remember, it takes all three categories to make up 100 percent clear communication.

A Real-Life Example

> In my former job as an Emergency Department nurse, I was part of a team taking care of 40-something year old man. He had some chronic conditions that he knew could adversely affect the heart. He also knew that sometimes, the only warning a person has during a heart attack is in just "not feeling right."
>
> Well, he "didn't feel right" and came to the E.R. accompanied by friends. He was in no way panicking, but he was very concerned, and understandably so. His manner was subdued and serious. One of the nurses, attempting to help him relax and feel more comfortable by joking with him, was rebuked. Being a really good nurse and communicator, she did not take offense and adjusted her interaction accordingly.

COMMUNICATION IMPACT: THE VISUAL 55%

When everything was done that could be done for the man *(i.e. monitor hook-up, IV line, EKG, labs drawn and preliminary meds given,)* I noted he still had that "deer caught in the headlights" look about him. I stood at the end of his stretcher, looked into his eyes and reviewed out loud all we had just done to him. I then emphasized to him that he was in the right place to be helped and that he was safe here and was going to be okay.

My eye contact and body language, coupled with careful audio communication *(emphasizing tone and tempo)* as I spoke words in complete alignment with my intention to help him relax and trust ... was all it took to decrease the man's feeling of impending doom. He visibly relaxed and allowed his perception of reality to include the possibility of a more positive outcome.

Practice Practice Practice

The reason I was able to work with 100 percent communication impact is because I know how I look, how I sound, and what words to use. I know this because I have practiced this until it has become second nature to me. It is second nature to me to know what I present outwardly. You will be amazed and pleased at your own effectiveness when this becomes second nature to you too!

Here's how:

Take a mental helicopter ride up to the ceiling. Look at yourself reading this book. Notice the environment around you ... the chair or couch ... the light.... Look at yourself. How are you sitting ... or are you lying down? Look more closely at your body position, your facial expression.

> *Looking down from my own helicopter position right now, I notice that my lips and the muscles around my mouth are pursed. As soon as I recognize that, I feel myself automatically relaxing those muscles.*

Repeat this practice of observing yourself in different situations throughout your day. Become comfortable with self-observation. Just as monitoring your self-talk is the beginning of becoming comfortable with self-reflection, monitoring your body is the beginning of becoming comfortable with self-observation. This kind of thinking and observing yourself while communicating helps you avoid after-thoughts laced with regret.

Go ahead. Practice these new skills in your next encounter with a colleague or someone significant in your life. Listen to your inner monologue *(self-reflect)*. Observe your body and your audible presentation. Then, armed with this knowledge, begin adjusting your three areas of communication impact so that your intention impacts the receiver 100 percent congruently!

Practice makes perfect

Let a colleague know how much you appreciate him or her. Let your significant other know how much you care. Positively impact the stranger you are serving ... or who may be serving you. As you make a conscious

COMMUNICATION IMPACT: THE VISUAL 55%

effort to control your inner monologue, align your areas of impact and enlist the help of the "six honest serving men," you'll be amazed at the level of response you begin to attract.

While most of the people around you are struggling to understand and be understood, *you* are now coming into your power. You are learning life skills that are going to set you above the rest.

A Note About Speed

We want to be seen as quick, decisive and intelligent. We mistakenly think we need to be this way in our encounters with other people. We think that if we are slow to respond, we'll be thought of as doltish and dumb.

Here's a news flash: When you give a thought-filled, measured response, others have the perception that you have fully paid attention to them. If you choose to practice this skill, you will join an elite minority of people who are in control of their communication and thus in control of their present and future!

A True Story

Here is another real life example of what practicing and becoming proficient in communication impact will do for you.

> Since 1997, I have traveled extensively giving seminars. I would be on the road one week out of each month.

My routine was that I'd arrive at a city, give a seminar, pack up and leave that city and then arrive at another city that evening to spend the night. The next day, I'd give a seminar in that city, pack up and leave, then arrive at the next city to spend the night. *(You get the idea.)*

Anyone who often travels knows what a nightmare "guaranteed" hotel reservations can become. In all my years of traveling, I only had two occasions where the hotel had given my "guaranteed" room away before I arrived. In both cases, the hotel offered to pay for a room and the cab fare to and from another hotel. Normally, I would have taken them up on it. *(Hey, it was a free room and a free ride!)* But in this instance, I was giving a seminar at their hotel. Once you start adding variables, chances for things to go wrong increase exponentially. I mean, if they had rented out a guaranteed room, might they also manage to rent out my seminar meeting room? *(In one case, my meeting room was double booked, and I ended up presenting my seminar to more than 100 people in the hotel lobby!)* Plus — what if the taxi back to their hotel on the morning of the seminar was late ... or had a wreck? I'd made a commitment to have my seminar on time and be effective.

So ... there I was at the hotel where my seminar was to take place the following day. The staff tells me my room has been booked, and there is nothing they can do.

Even though I was in the right with guaranteed reservations in hand, I knew that losing my temper would serve no purpose. Still, my intent was to stay right there and spend the night in the hotel where I

Communication Impact: The Visual 55%

was hosting the next day's seminar. Here's what I did. I remained visually open, calm and sincerely smiling. My voice conveyed the dilemma we were in, but remained upbeat, not sarcastic. This was the content:

> "I know you said there is no one to call and nothing you can do. I strongly suggest that all of you put your heads together and figure out how to get me a sleeping room here tonight. I'm not leaving. I'm not causing a disturbance. I have papers in hand proving a guaranteed reservation. I welcome you to call a supervisor who will help you to solve this problem. I do not mind if you call the police, because that would only help my case in court, because of the fraudulent practice of not delivering on our contract. It would also help with the lawsuit regarding the seminar that will be cancelled tomorrow. Be heroes and solve this problem, avoid the lawsuit, maintain goodwill and keep our future business."

What happened? I got my room. They told me an assistant manager gave up his room just for me. I think this information was supposed to make me feel bad. It didn't. I found out later why they were willing to send me across town and pay all my expenses. The semi-annual bar exam was being held there, and they had rented rooms at quadruple their customary rate.

The point is, how do you call police and forcibly remove someone who is smiling, not causing a disturbance, and has paperwork proving his contractual rights? If I had been demonstrative, loud and sarcastic, then the primary problem would be "me." I would lose.

8 Keys To Connecting

Fun Pastime

Begin to notice what visual acts others are doing during conversations. Do their words match up with their facial expressions, posture or other visible actions? When a person is telling you he wants to stay and chat, but his body has been angled away from you and he's been leaning toward the door from the first second of meeting you and his movements have been quick and jerky, is this visual impact telling you he wants to stay? No way!

You may ask, *"Isn't he just being sociable — as much as his time allows?"* My rejoinder to that is, *"Perhaps, but he should be truthful. He shouldn't half-step or sugar coat it. He comes off as phony, manipulative and demeaning of your evaluation capability."*

If someone wants to stay but cannot, it must be verbalized. If one doesn't want to stay, but is trying to convince you otherwise, good luck! When you are aware of the 100% breakdown, you won't be fooled.

We tend to think that if we make warm, friendly statements, we'll be liked, appreciated and understood. But how can someone understand you when you are saying one thing and physically acting out another?

You may ask, *"But what if you really do want to chat, but can't due to a prior commitment?"* Begin with that! Verbalize what your body is communicating anyway!

> "You've probably noticed that I appear rushed, and I am."

COMMUNICATION IMPACT: THE VISUAL 55%

That's not being dismissive. You're actually acknowledging another's innate ability — consciously or subconsciously — to correctly evaluate what's going on with you. Only someone with extreme low self esteem or poor self-image will take offense.

Being consciously aware of how you look and sound and of the words you use gives you amazing control over your communications events. It is similar to what actors must accomplish. An actor can have great lines to say and deliver them with the correct tone of voice, but if the visible actions are incongruent with the tone and the words, it all comes across flat.

Lights ... Camera ...

Stanislavsky, a Russian theatrical director and coach, always stressed the importance of not acting the part, but of **being** the part. If the scene calls for you to be searching for a ring you misplaced, then truly put yourself in the mind-set of *"I've misplaced my ring, and I need to find it!"* Go about looking as if you really did lose your ring — a cherished, important ring. Search as if your life depends on it. Your mind cannot hold two opposite thoughts simultaneously. If you try, the mental vacillation will come across as hollow, not true. The effect will be neutral. However, when your mind is singular in purpose, it is conveyed outwardly and perceived as true.

> **Writing this has just brought to mind two classic statements:**

8 Keys To Connecting

"Know thyself." — *Socrates*

"To thine own self be true."
— *Shakespeare*

Perceived Appearance

Let's take a moment to discuss body language. Books have been written on the subject which you may choose to explore. For now, just be mindful that in communication encounters, our perceived appearance can include facial expression, body posture *(open or closed,)* direction of the feet *(toward or away,)* and the direction in which we are leaning *(toward or away.)* All these factors convey non-verbal messages. These messages can be incongruent with what we are saying and how we are saying it.

For Example ...

We are open and smiling warmly, but we have a hand on the doorknob and are leaning toward the exit. In this example, the occasion to *"know thyself"* and *"to thine own self be true"* would be by owning up outwardly by verbalizing...

> "I've got to run."

If this sounds trivial, then answer this question. Did you feel welcomed and appreciated the last time you went into a fast food restaurant, when, upon entering, every employee within twenty-feet of the door said,

COMMUNICATION IMPACT: THE VISUAL 55%

"*Hi! Welcome!*" and upon leaving, the same employees within a twenty-foot zone chorused, "*Thank you and come back soon!*"?

Forced Feels Fake

I once worked in a hospital which instituted the six-foot rule. All employees who were in the halls, stairways, and elevators were to greet anyone who passed within six feet of them. As a result of this "forced niceness," the greetings were abrupt and reactionary in tone which fell far short of the genuine, spontaneous hospitality it was supposed to produce. The areas of communication impact were highly incongruent within and among themselves, thus few were fooled by this mandated niceness.

The late Jim Rohn, speaker, author, consultant, and all-around brilliant business person, talked about the company that advertised the following; "*We don't train our people to be nice. We hire nice people.*" An all-time successful airline, regardless of the market ups and downs, Southwest, is known for its friendly and fun employees. They work in an environment where they are given control of how they treat the customer, just so long as it is friendly and creates customer loyalty. One can imagine all the potential problems from that, due to the fact that what I consider friendly and fun is most likely different than what you would identify with. But that is not necessarily so. My belief – recently supported by Daniel Goleman's research published in Primal Leadership and Social Intelligence – is that we as humans are more alike than not, regardless of gender, age, culture, and economics. We're hard-wired in our brains and respond similarly – as can be shown by an MRI – when posed with specific situations.

Let's get back to Southwest Airlines ...

How can a company loosen the reins on so many different people in order to allow them to create an atmosphere of friendliness and fun? Easy – screen them at the front end. People who are already customer service oriented are hired. But what happens when someone else has more technical experience, or more years of experience, or knows someone who knows someone, etc. So far the dominant ethos is to hire for personality traits which display genuine customer service. All the experience and technical know how can be learned. Besides, technical know how is challenged every eighteen months to two years due to new technical systems being installed. An out-going, positive, self-starting, excellent communicator has more capability of learning new systems than someone who fails in these attributes.

But don't people put on their "best" when applying for a job? Yes, and that is why a series of interviews coupled with seemingly unrelated social interactions should be evaluated. You luncheon with a prospect. How does the prospect act toward the waiter or waitress, the bus boy, the older person holding up the line while digging for the exact change? How does the applicant act toward other applicants during coffee and donut breaks or when another applicant has to stand up in front of the group and tell why they want to work there? Genuine, outwardly displayed, positive regard for another person

COMMUNICATION IMPACT: THE VISUAL 55%

indicates customer service know how. That is why Southwest is the only airline that has always been in the black financially. They know real customer service!

What This Book Is And Is Not ...

This book is about building mutually satisfying relationships, be they with customers, employees, teachers, friends, peers or others. It's not about saving the world or being a social therapist to those who may need one.

... And A Caution

I also want to address what I refer to as *"the herd of one."* They are the needy, the never satisfied, the manipulators, the always finagling, and the trouble makers who consistently corrupt situations.

Herd of One

Humans are social beings. Mentally healthy humans enjoy the company of others. The most stringent punishment in the prison system is solitary confinement. So it is true that to be without companionship is painful.

Now enter 'the herd of one'. I use this metaphor from the fact horses are herd animals. They require the rest of the herd, even if it is only one other, to be present before they can relax. A solitary horse is nervous, easily spooked, and should be reunited as soon as possible with their own kind.

The herd of one in human terms prefers isolation

> to companionship. That is the extreme. On the road to isolation one can detect the degrees of progress: fault finding with everyone and everything, no time for social activities, attempts to stir up strife when none is present, and an overall cynicism of life.
>
> If you are a rescuer type person – beware. These types can take you down with them. And keep in mind we are influenced by those we spend time with. Out of necessity to continue being with someone we exhibit their actions, attitudes, and beliefs. Some people enjoy being miserable and they will take down any who attempt to thwart their misery. "Pain in life is inevitable; misery is optional."

Jim Rohn, the business & life philosopher we referenced earlier had this to share regards how he and his wife lived: *"I'll take care of me for you and you take care of you for me"*. There will be times when others need your help and this is good to give that help. But if that becomes a constant, and is predominately one way that is not good. And if their view of life is negative, cynical, and melancholy that is not good for you either.

Take care of you first so that you can be of help to others when needed, and keep an attitude of gratitude because when tallied, far more good happens to us who live in America and similar countries than in emerging nations. Here's a reply that Dave Ramsey, radio host & financial peace creator , uses when asked, *"How are you?"* he replies, *"Better than I deserve!"*

Now that's a keeper!

Chapter 4

Auditory 38%: It's How you Sound

"Lower your voice and strengthen your argument." — Lebanese Proverb

The second-most important perception is how you sound. The words *"I love you"* can only have an impact when the sound you give them has certain qualities. There is a term – flat affect – which applies both to visual and auditory perception. Flat affect, visually, means without expression – a doll-like countenance. Flat affect, auditorily, means without inflection in voice – a monotone. A good example would be when the old sci-fi movies would have a robot talking. It was a flat monotone, with no change in speed of delivery. Do any of these descriptions bring to mind people with whom you have dealt? If while on the phone, you've heard a flat monotone, as if scripted greeting, how do you respond? I have fun with them, and I'll say *"I'll bet you can't say that three times quickly without making a mistake."* Some laugh, and then I am dealing with a human. Some don't, and I have to decide if I want to work very hard

Auditory 38%: Its How You Sound

and get help from this person – with the foreknowledge that I have only a 50% chance of success.

The Importance of Sound

Sound is extremely important. In fact, with some people, sound is more important than appearance. But the general rule is that the visual impacts most, and then the auditory comes in at a close second. It is not the degree of aesthetics or beauty. Beauty is in the eye of the beholder. Rather, it is in the degree of congruency. Is what you see coming across as true? And then, is what you see congruent, in alignment, with what the voice sounds like?

This is where comedy situations can be manufactured – where part of what is seen is incongruent with other

8 Keys To Connecting

visual aspects, and the sound of the voice is incongruent with what is seen, as well as what is being said. Laurel & Hardy and Abbott & Costello are good examples of comedic incongruity in communication.

Sarcasm can be picked up immediately, just by the sound or tone of voice. We have all been on both sides – the giving and receiving of sarcasm; and it is all in the sound.

Sound can be neutral, but that is different from being flat. Sound can express concern, but that is different from being empathetic. Sound can convey displeasure, but that is different from anger. Sarcasm can traverse across all emotions and delivery types while totally lacking sincerity. Before we go on to actual content, I want to address the absence of sound – the pause, or silence – one of the most powerful aspects of sound.

AUDITORY 38%: ITS HOW YOU SOUND

When someone is talking to us, we have a tendency to race ahead of what they are saying and begin constructing our reply. We fill in the blanks, our ever-efficient mind leaping ahead to what we think they are going to say. We wish to impress through wit, word and wizardry. As soon as they finish, sometimes even before they finish, we take the stage and proclaim.

Dale Carnegie, author of *How to Win Friends and Influence People*, states the most influential tack one can take is to be impressed – not to impress. The way of accomplishing this is to really listen to what a person is saying — to actually become a sponge taking it in. And when they are finished, be silent – for a minimum count of three. The pause extends in a very real perceived way that you are giving thought to what you have just heard. Don't try to fake it. They will know shortly, through your comments and questions, whether you were really listening. After you pause — then and only then — do you begin the construct of your reply.

> **To be heard is one thing, but to be listened to and asked questions for understanding – that is the ultimate compliment.**

This is not for all encounters. A chance meeting in an elevator or fast food restaurant is an example of such encounters that do not require a large degree of depth in communication. But far too many interpersonal communication events are not afforded the elegance of the pause. Practice it. Use it often. Start giving another human being the ultimate compliment: listening for understanding.

> Go to an auction and listen to how the bids are solicited. An undulating voice, speedily encouraging competitive bidding from the audience, creating an atmosphere of excitement, challenge; *"I won the bid!"*

The sound creates a tempo which, the auctioneer hopes will stop rational thinking and maximize audience participation in raising the bid. The sound is the essential ingredient.

> Picture yourself addressing a large group of people. You have what you will say in writing in front of you. You are dressed exactly right, your hair is perfect. Visually you are perfect. You begin to speak and ...

Regardless of how you filled in the blank, you know that how you sound will either add to or detract from your presentation. At this point the sound is the essential ingredient.

> You are with a group of people you want to impress or a special someone in the group. Visually you are in synch - you open your mouth and ...

Once again, sound is the essence of impression at that moment.

Three entirely different situations but sound is essential in each. So how does one take control of how they sound? It's easy to do but a little difficult to remember. The difficult part has to do with habits of doing. It is rare for anyone to be taught the skill of controlling how they sound.

AUDITORY 38%: ITS HOW YOU SOUND

I was told, innumerable times, *"You better watch that tone of voice."* Now that's specific enough but it never dawned on me that sound of voice alone can help or hinder in a profound way. When I finally realized the power of the sound of my voice I started getting better results in my communication. The results were more predictable and this alone led me to become more skilled in "*how I sound.*"

How to Take Control of Sound

Speed of response ...

I am not talking about getting or giving direction, or giving or receiving orders. I am talking about those times when you want to be remembered. The speed of your response affects the sound. A thoughtful *(thought filled)* response requires time. A flippant reply does not. Which one will serve you best?

Clarity of words ...

Do your words run together or are they distinct and clear? This is not to be confused with regional accents. There is an elegance to be found in each region's accent and in no way affects understanding of speech. Be clear in your pronunciation of words but don't eliminate your accent. It adds to your uniqueness.

Volume ...

Do you adjust to your surroundings or is it always a challenge to hear you? Be aware of your listener's ability to hear you. If in doubt – ask.

8 Keys To Connecting

Breath ...

> The depth of your breath affects the depth of your voice. Breathe deep into your abdomen to add depth and timber to your voice. Abdominal breathing, where you see the belly rise and fall, is healthier and it adds to the impact of your sound. Chest breathing is shallow and causes a shallow sound to your voice. Shallow is easily ignored and dismissed.

Emotion and Emphasis

Pausing and emphasizing a word or phrase signals your listener in a way that clarifies your intention. Monotone, stagnant cadence puts people to sleep or they drift off into mentally making their grocery list.

> ***Emotion is to voice what spice is to food, percussion is to calypso, dance is to human form.***

Use emotion in your voice to show that what you are speaking about matters. But be careful – do not be too emotional lest your listener 'tune out'. Saying more will cause less!

Finally, to reiterate, I will bring up sarcasm. Both Latin and Greek, it is derived from 'tearing of flesh'! It garners many different emotions: It is a form of bullying.

Everyone on the scene is impacted:

> *The deliverer feels self adulation, pride, condescension.*
>
> *The receiver feels self loathing, anger, depression.*
>
> *The observer feels fear.*

Auditory 38%: Its How You Sound

When you use sarcasm it makes you feel superior, quick witted and momentarily in the spot light of victory!

Sarcasm is a club, or bullet, used by any and all types. It is very addictive. The ignorant use it often not realizing how it closes off many opportunities. The mean spirited use it when they know it won't ambush them later. An excellent communicator uses it rarely and even then only as a means of communicating how not to speak or behave.

Chapter 5

Content 7%: Small but Powerful

"In three words I can sum up everything I've learned about life: It goes on." — **Robert Frost**

Do not let the 7 percent of communication comprised of actual content fool you into not paying enough attention to its detail. The difference between one word and another can be the difference between a sale or not, a relationship or not, permission or not.

You are seen first and evaluated, then heard and evaluated, and then your words are listened to and weighed. And in the weighing, you are found either worthy or wanting.

A person's vocabulary is not just an indication of their education. It also creates access to different emotions. A limited vocabulary limits your emotions, as well as limiting the emotions you evoke in another person. If a person only expresses being happy or angry, there is no "in between." Another way to express this would

Content 7%: Small But Powerful

be; if all you have are hot and cold, and no warm, tepid or cool, you are stuck with only extremes. One must increase his or her vocabulary in order to have access to variables and nuances in emotions and access to another person's range of emotions.

It is very important that you realize you can influence another's range of emotions by providing the right words. To be perturbed is nowhere near anger and does not imply agreement or neutrality. To be disappointed does not make you out as being upset, but it also does not categorize you as being OK with whatever is at issue. Being amused is not doing back flips and is not anywhere near being bored.

> *Get a thesaurus. Begin with the basic emotions such as being happy, fearful, angry, sad, and joyful. Begin to use, when appropriate, the attending words that delineate a feeling along the continuum of human expression. Learn new words, not for the purpose of impressing, but for the purpose of being precise.*

"Hegemony" imparts information more precisely than "leading influential nations." "Celebrate" imparts more ideas than "good time." "Elegiac" is a bit much, unless speaking with someone who is immersed in literary romanticism. Similarly, when speaking to a veteran of a war zone, military or civilian, referring to the emotional numbness resulting from seeing repeated mutilation and death will ring true in a deeper, more profound sense than in speaking thus to one who has not lived these experiences. But using such words will give even the neophyte a glimpse of that reality.

The majority of your words must be within the realm of the listener's repertoire. Usual and customary wins friends, whereas multi-syllabic, multiple nuanced meanings in the dictionary, or two separate groups claiming theirs as the proper pronunciation, will erect barriers.

Right about now, some might be saying, *"He starts off telling us to use the thesaurus and then tells us to back off from using it."* And you are right, but here is the distinction. Always communicate with this simultaneous intent: to make understanding easy for the recipient, yet honor them by giving a detailed description spanning the full range of human experience.

Jim Rohn, speaker, author, businessman, and noted authority, tells about a group of friends who did a study probing why violent criminals did what they did. One resulting opinion after the study was *"limited vocabulary."* If the only choice they had was between happy or mad, then the actions they took were dependant on referenced emotions. Happy or mad leaves no room for frustrated, displeased, or neutral.

CONTENT 7%: SMALL BUT POWERFUL

Give due diligence to your word and phrasing choices. Stay clear of sarcasm both in tone and word. Be clear in your mind that your intention is to be understood, without making the listener labor to understand your meanings. And finally, pay tribute to human language. Use all that is available to your knowledge, yet maintain regard to the listener's ability to understand what you say.

In our day to day lives there is repetition of events. You often see the same people engaging in the same activities and with the same attitude.

For Example, you arrive at work and greet your colleagues. Previously your routine was visually flat, auditorily flat and content flat.

You want different results in your life? Begin where you are most familiar. Work and school are highly predictable so start there.

Chapter 3 helps with your visual, Chapter 4 with your sound and now let's do content.

What is usually asked?	*What is the Usual Reply?*
Hi, how are you?	Fine.
Good Morning.	Morning.
What's happening?	Nothing.

8 Keys To Connecting

Now Let's Try These ...

You are asked:	You Reply:
Hi, how are you?	Living the dream. How about you? -or- Better than good. Better than most. And you?

Try them. See the results you get. Now you are becoming memorable. But do you do this with people you have just met?

This is where discernment enters. Don't be cute and don't distinguish yourself this way. The tried and true is best here. The environment or event you are greeting this person in will determine the words to use.

New Business:

>Hi, glad to meet you.
>
>Hi, how are you?
>
>Thank you for meeting with me. How are you today?

New Acquaintances:

>Glad to meet you. My name is ____. And you are? *(make it about them)*

CONTENT 7%: SMALL BUT POWERFUL

Serious or Somber Event:

My name is ─────.
May I help you?
Can I help you?
Please let me know if there is something I can do for you.

Serious and New: (new for them – but you do this every day, i.e. nurse, doctor, police, complaint dept.)

My name is ─────.
This is not every day for you.
This is upsetting.
This might be scary, I know it would be for me.

8 Keys To Connecting

Vocabulary

The more vocabulary you have to choose from gives the more ability to describe, define and direct the course of conversations. An easy way to increase your vocabulary is to learn new words through the context of their use. Reading non-fiction or higher echelon fiction will make the words easier to remember.

> "The jury's ennui was surpassed only by the judge's napping during the cross examination."

'Boredom' could have been used instead of 'ennui' but when you wish to highlight an atmosphere the use of ennui *(higher echelon)* and the use of napping *(a common term)* highlights a situation. When you look the word up for its meaning the context of use will anchor it in your memory.

Use the Word a Week in the Resources section on my website. Go to the library and peruse their magazine section. By the way, look up peruse, its definition will surprise you.

Chapter 6

How People Process Information

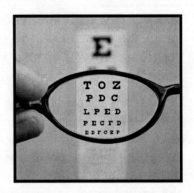

"Some people learn by watching, some learn by listening and some have to take it apart and put it together. They're all good in their fashion." — *Anonymous*

Neuro-Linguistic Programming

Neuro-Linguistic Programming *(NLP)* is a multi-faceted study about why and how people behave. It is a fascinating investigation of human behavior. Here is a brief overview but make time to investigate it in depth. *Instant Rapport* by Michael Brooks is a good resource.

Changing another person's perception through word descriptions, sound and rhythm of voice and connecting to them in a way they are comfortable with is one of the skills derived from Neuro-Linguistic Programming.

Connecting what is happening to the person at this moment in time with what you want them to learn,

How People Process Information

accept, do, or experience is making what you are suggesting *(as in learn, accept, do or experience)* more credible. How? Because you are linking it to what is really happening to the person.

An example ...

As you sit and read these words and sentences and paragraphs and understand the sense and the logic and the truth of what they convey it becomes easier and easier for you to communicate with almost anyone, anywhere, on anything. Read, absorb, practice and own these skills while you sit and read this book. Enjoy the pleasure of getting better and better every day in every way.

> *This chapter will only deal with one facet of NLP: how people most comfortably process incoming information.*

Humans have five senses: seeing, hearing, touching, tasting and smelling. Most use all, though some have access only to a few. In NLP one tenet is that if a person has access to all five senses, then one of these senses will be the dominant one in how they process incoming information.

A person is either dominant in the visual, auditory, or kinesthetic *(touch and feeling)* area.

> **Visual people** process incoming information through a reference of colors, lines, shapes or succinctly put – in pictures.

8 Keys To Connecting

Auditory people process incoming information through sound, rhythm and volume. Alliteration *(using 3 words together that all begin with the same sound or letter: i.e. A Minor Matter of Murder)* is heaven sent to an auditory.

Kinesthetic people process incoming information through handling it, getting a feel *of* or *for* it. Showing or talking just doesn't do it for a kinesthetic. *"Hand that to me. I want to get a feel for it"* is what they will say to you.

A person who is dominant auditorily will look at a map and be overwhelmed. They need the directions provided out loud. Give them a GPS with spoken directions and they are content. *A visually dominant person* will listen to directions, but relies on a map to be able to ascertain general directions, streets and landmarks to reference. *The kinesthetic dominant person* would love to have been able to make the map, but suffices with touching, folding, and marking on the map.

This is by no means an in-depth study regarding the ***visual-auditory-kinesthetic*** *(**VAK**) processing of information. This is a "bare bones" overview. In biology class, when they provided the anatomy of anything, it usually began with just the bones. Then the muscles, tendons, ligaments, and other parts were added. This section is about the major bones only. Applicable – yes. Nuanced and sophisticated – no.*

"Maps and directions" is one example of differences in processing information. Another good example would be married people. A conversation between an auditory lady and a visual man might go ...

How People Process Information

Wife :

"You never say you love me."

Husband :

"I say it by the size of that rock on your finger."

Now, optimally, each would consider how the other predominantly processes information and provide it in the form of the other person's preference. I happen to be auditory, whereas my wife, Charlotte, is visual. I attribute our continuation to our understanding of this difference, and to our periodically providing the other's preference.

Here is the key for you to use this knowledge to make the other person comfortable in processing your communication to them. Listen to what they say. Note exactly what dominates in their speech.

8 Keys To Connecting

Are they saying …

"I can see that," "Can you make the idea more clear?" "It's shrouded in grays," or "Can you paint a picture for me to understand?"

— OR —

"It doesn't ring true," "I don't hear it," "It pops," "It doesn't sound right," "It sounds right," It's a melody," or "It's harmonious."

— OR —

"I don't get it," "It doesn't feel right," "It feels OK," "My gut says no," "I feel I/we should do it," or "It touched me."

When you listen for these indicators and then serve back in the same sense, then you are making it easier for that person to understand you. You are also building a bridge. Subliminally, they are deciding you are like them. And people like people who are like themselves.

If you can't discern their dominant style, then serve back using all the different senses. This will make your communication richer, fuller, and more aligned with everyone. You will be more interesting, naturally.

Chapter 7

Four Personality Types

"If a man is as wise as a serpent, he can afford to be as harmless as a dove."
— **Cheyenne Proverb**

Have you ever noticed specific traits attached to individuals and then noticed those traits can be generally seen in other individuals as well? I am not talking about neurotic traits such as obsessive cleanliness, obsessive orderliness, or obsessing about remembering if you locked the door, or turned off the iron, coffee pot, or any sundry bit of things. I am talking about different personality types of people such as the person who is predominantly concerned with the "bottom line;" a general overview of what is needed and what the expected gain or results will be. Then there are people who want the minutiae, all the variables and all the tangential possible outcomes; those who view more data as wonderful, not a distraction. Still another group are those who predominantly worry about people; their safety, security, and happiness. Finally, there is the type

Four Personality Types

who is a fun-loving, a big picture, "let the games begin" type person.

What I have described are four basic personality types. I was first made aware of these by Tony Alessandra, Ph.D. He is one of the rare academics who can take a concept and explain it so we average mortals can understand it and use it to our benefit. I highly recommend his books and his audio programs from Nightingale/Conant Audio Tapes. Not only are they entertaining, but also very useful.

Dr. Alessandra developed a visual that is helpful in understanding the four personality types. If you take a square piece of paper and fold it in half, fold it in half again, then open it up you will have a four quadrant grid. The personality types as outlined by Dr. Alessandra have very specific places on the grid. Dr. Alessandra titles one personality type the Director and places it in the lower right quadrant. In the lower left quadrant Dr. Alessandra places the Thinker personality type. The upper left quadrant is where he places the Relater. Finally he places the Socializer in the upper right quadrant. Dr. Alessandra intentionally places types with opposing traits diagonal to each other. The Relater is diagonal to the Director. The Socializer is diagonal from the Thinker.

If you have drawn out the grid thus far, there are only two more defining characteristics. Write the word OPEN across the top of the grid to encompass the Relater and Socializer. Write the word CLOSED across the bottom of the grid to encompass the Director and Thinker. Then, write the word DIRECT down the right hand side of the grid to encompass the Director and Socializer. Finally, write the word INDIRECT down the left side of the grid to encompass the Relater and Thinker. This completes Dr. Alessandra's four general personality types grid.

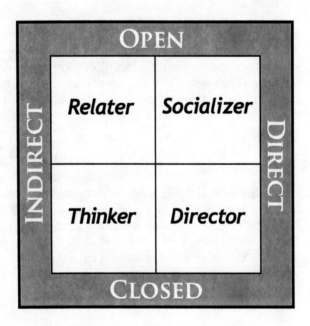

You already know them ...

In my seminars I tell everyone they already know the different personality styles just from their environment. I then prove it to them through comparisons of the environments of the different types.

Four Personality Types

The Director ...

is predominantly concerned with the bottom line; profit/loss; project completion. A Director will have the door to his or her office closed. You need to make an appointment to talk with them. Their desk will be clean, barren, and big.

The Relater ...

is predominantly concerned with people's welfare. A Relater's office door will be open. You can pop in without an appointment. In fact, they may think there is a serious problem if you make an appointment. Their desk will have pictures, candy, flowers, and a box of tissues.

The Socializer ...

has a "big picture" penchant. A Socializer's door will be open. They may be in the office or they may be out talking with others. In a conversation with a Socializer they want to talk about themselves, what they are doing, what big events are coming up, etc. Their desk will have a calendar of events, vacation plans, and personal awards or accomplishments.

The Thinker ...

is concerned with detail and logical progression. The Thinker's door will be closed. An appointment is required because it must be scheduled. A Thinker's desk is covered with graphs and books upon books of reference such as statistics, logic, research, and theory. If you want something done right, give it to a Thinker. However, if you want it done on time – think again!

8 Keys To Connecting

But ... which am I?

It might be confusing because you will recognize yourself in more than one category. You might be thinking, *"Hey, I'm a Thinker when I need to be and I'm a Socializer when it calls for that. I can relate to people with genuine concern, but when it is needed, I direct in order to keep things moving."* We all have parts of all four personality types and we display what is most appropriate according to the occasion. However, each of us has a dominant type, a safe haven; a type that we feel has served us well. Our dominant style appears most forcefully when we are sick, tired, angry or afraid. When a person is stressed and feeling overwhelmed, that is when the dominant type takes over.

Under stress ...

A Director ... will display more control

A Relater ... will display more concern for everyone

A Socializer ... will retreat into focusing beyond the stress

A Thinker ... will delve deeper into the "why" of the stress and how to neutralize it.

When you know your dominant type, then you can choose to be in control of your tendencies toward that type. Remember that having a self-awareness and conscious control will serve you best. Directing others forcefully without concern will get you abject obedience or it will incite revolt. Conversely, worrying about one's welfare without thought toward goals and mission serves no one ultimately. Ignoring the immediate problem and only thinking about good times is not realistic. Analyzing to the exclusion of everyone, including self, will cause burn out.

The dominant type does serve well, but if it is allowed to govern you to the exclusion of the other three, then you will find yourself more often alone. In fact, if you go too deeply into the one type, you will find that even others who have the same dominant type as you will avoid you. Your personality will be a caricature and you will be the subject of amusement for others at your expense. Be conscious and aware and that will put you in control.

How do you find your dominant type?

One way is to take inventory of your actions especially when you are sick, tired, angry, or afraid. An honest self-appraisal will show the type you feel most comfortable with. Another, and perhaps more telling way is to evaluate the people who most irritate or frustrate you. Once you find their dominant type – yours will be diagonally opposite on the grid.

There is another skill to learn with regard to personality types that will enhance your relationship building with nearly everyone. The adage "birds of a feather flock together" is very true. People like people who are like themselves.

In relationship building, when you become consciously aware of yourself in all your communication modes you will also be consciously aware of others' tendencies, traits, and proclivities. Ralph Waldo Emerson is attributed with saying *"Everything about you is screaming so loudly I can't hear what you're saying."* What he is referring to is that we communicate so much of who we are through actions, adornment, and mannerisms.

It is important for you to begin the assessment and evaluation of the person you are communicating with in regards to their dominant type. Their environment, attitude, and mannerisms will help, and your evaluation of them will be confirmed when they open up towards you. You assess them as a director and act accordingly. If you are correct, you will be thought of as being like them. And it bears repeating; people like people who are like themselves.

There is one final polish to this skill and strategy of personality types: I will share it through the following example. At the end of this section in my seminar I put forth the following scenario to the group:

> You have just purchased another company and have merged your present company with the new one because they have similar products, services, and can compliment the overall business success. You know one way to get people from both companies on board toward the goal of team building is to institute the first annual picnic. You pick a Socializer personality and a Thinker personality to plan and execute delivery of the picnic. The question is: what kind of picnic will you have?

Four Personality Types

I get two different responses from the audience. One is you might not have a picnic, and the other is you'll have the best picnic ever. This is one of the rare occasions when both answers could be right.

"No picnic" could be the right answer if the two opposite personalities do not understand where the other is coming from and instead view the other person as being an irritating boor.

If the two do understand where the other person is coming from, the outcome is quite different. If they evaluate the other's personality type, interpret the communication through that lens, and act accordingly, then you will have the best picnic ever.

Read the following communication exchange between a Socializer and a Thinker who are in charge of the annual picnic. These two do understand how the other one thinks and acts.

The Socializer : *(big picture)*

"We'll have a band."

The Thinker : *(minutiae)*

"We need shelter or a rain date. We need to get the demographics to see what music will be most liked ..."

8 Keys To Connecting

The Socializer : *(big picture)*

"Yes, yes, you take care of that and let's have a stand up comic."

The Thinker : *(minutiae)*

"Are the children coming? According to their ages we have to evaluate the comedian's material."

The Socializer : *(big picture)*

"Yes, yes, you've got that and speaking of kids; maybe pony rides, too."

The Thinker : *(minutiae)*

"Let's find out the age ranges and their numbers ..."

If the two in the previous example did not understand their opposite type, the communication would have digressed into accusing each other of being difficult, or being negative, or too "whatever."

Understanding different personality types, working within their perspective and using the qualities of all four types in the optimal context will make you able to get along with almost everyone and in almost all situations. Talk about control over your destiny! You will no longer think of people as being lucky. You will know that luck is really an acronym meaning Laboring Under Correct Knowledge. So go get lucky!

Chapter 8

The Right Impact vs the Almost Right

"What counts can't always be counted. What can be counted doesn't always count."
— Albert Einstein

So far we have covered face to face communication. In this chapter we'll cover the disappearing social grace known as; the thank you note and the snail mail letter.

The email, phone call, or twitter alert have their uses, but they are not a panacea to all situations regardless of their convenience. And that's exactly why their use is limited in their impact – their convenience. The short email sent even if loaded with appropriate, high-sounding, warm, fuzzy adjectives brings with it a picture of the sender checking off an item from the long list of "things to do soon." It is the drive through at a fast food restaurant versus the planned dinner date which requires reservations. It is the search for a gift that shows the receiver "you noted what is important to them." When

The Right Impact vs the Almost Right

you send the card or letter you are not just sending a 44 cent snail mail piece of paper. Here is what you are sending. The mental image of you picking out the card, sitting at a table, removing all random thoughts from your stream of consciousness, focusing solely on the recipient, possibly test writing some thoughts on scratch paper, selecting the apropos, committing it to paper, in your finest script, sealing it in the envelope, addressing it, possibly with an artistic flair, selecting, not just the run of the mill generic stamp, but one that supports your intent or speaks to a mutually held admiration and then entrusting it to the U.S. Postal Service for safe, assured delivery. That's the kind of impact you're sending. Mark Twain once wrote; "The difference between the almost right word & the right word is really a large matter--it's the difference between the lightning bug and the lightning." I can't top that analogy. I can only say "ditto" regards email, phone call, twitter alert and the handwritten note or letter. When you want to be memorable spend the money and time.

8 Keys To Connecting

What else does it take to be memorable?

First is the sincere desire to connect to another person in your communication. What makes this possible is putting the other person first. This is accomplished through the skillful asking of questions all about them in a way they predominantly process information *(VAK)* and in a style *(4 personality styles)* they are most comfortable with.

Zig Ziglar, speaker, author, and business philosopher had a wonderful saying *"help enough other people get what they want and you'll definitely get what you want."*

Everyone wants to be recognized and understood.

There's a whole industry that has grown immensely due to that need *(psychotherapy)*. When a person feels recognized and understood there occurs a significant event. It is called psychological reciprocity. This is where they naturally want to recognize and understand you. *(Now this excludes the 'herd of one' and the 'hooray for me to heck with everyone else' people.)* Excluding them, I have found most people will want to get to know you, understand you and even help you when they can. And this occurs nearly always when they experience it coming from you.

Do not become discouraged when you fail to make a connection. Who knows all of what is going on in another person's life. But as you practice and refine

The Right Impact vs the Almost Right

these skills and strategies you will minimize *(eventually neutralize)* any miscommunications on your part.

Ralph Waldo Emerson wrote, "If you want a friend then be a friend." What does it mean to be a friend? What is your definition of 'a friend'? And do you think of these qualities as coming from you or experienced by you?

This is a crucial distinction. The younger the child the more the reference is to "me first." Growing in maturity also means putting others first. *(No, not being a door mat.)*

In her book, *A Book of Courtesy*, Sister Mary Mercedes, O.P. writes: "One of the most helpful influences in our lives is a good friendship. ... A healthy friendship calls for what is best in us and stimulates us to our highest endeavors. ... The person who knows himself and his imperfections needs to be careful that it is not by his weaknesses that he attracts friends, but by his strengths."

Kate Zabriskie, owner of Business Training Works, and one who it can be said of 'Never met a stranger' represents the focused achiever. Her successful international business training company sets the standards in the industry of corporate training. Customer Service, Team Design and Development, Multi-National/Multi-Cultural Communication, Employee Development, Flexible Futures Business Design, are just a few of her company's customized training programs. Her specialized team of trainers, educators and consultants are the best of the best in getting results. I'm sharing this because Kate's successful longevity is a result of her excellence in communication.

8 Keys To Connecting

Communication Is Foundational

Poor or just 'okay' communication will not withstand the ups and downs of life. A conscious commitment to excellent communication will put you on an upward trajectory to success. These 8 chapters are the keys and used effectively will ensure your positive communication impact. *8 Keys To Connecting*, the book, is purposefully short. Its brevity provides a complete overview of all that needs work and refinement. Please do not stop here. Continue to read, practice and refine these skills I've shared with you. Use the website, contribute to the forum and join the self-selected few who have committed to becoming Excellent Communicators.

This is a challenge due to all the variables. It's like being a One-Man-Band, but there are great numbers who have successfully accomplished becoming Excellent Communicators.

Afterword

The quality of your questions will determine the quality of your life. You say to yourself, *"Okay, I've read the book-now what?"* Let's polish this question up a bit.

> *"What exactly should I do next in order to continue forward momentum in becoming an excellent communicator, learning how to make friends more easily, how to fit in, how to achieve and excel?"*

In a few words; use the web site, **www.8keys2connecting.com** or **www.8k2c.com**. Begin with the action plan and self-evaluation. Buy a blank calendar, make copies and start measuring your progress on one skill. When that skill becomes part of who you are *(this happens when you automatically begin evaluating yourself, your self-talk, in comparison to that skill)* then move on to the next skill and begin mapping it on a new calendar.

Read the 8 Keys To Connecting Blog. Comment on the blog posts. Watch the vignettes. Check out the book recommendations. Begin building your vocabulary with "Word for the Week" in the Resources section.

You are embarking on a journey that is going to open doors, provide opportunities and give you options that you never dreamed possible for yourself. Prepare to have a grand adventure!

Health & Joy to You,
Darren

"If I have seen further than others, it is by standing upon the shoulders of giants."

Upon the Shoulders of Giants

The following are in the order that I read them and do not imply numerical import. I believe the order is a clue toward the impact these authors had on me.

Albert Mehrabian Ph.D.
Silent Messages & Nonverbal Communication
  Two seperate works that are a foundation to the seminars I designed regards Interpersonal Communication.

S.I. Hayakawa U.S. Senator Hawaii *(an academic who studied semantics before becoming a U.S. senator)*
Language in Thought & Action
  A must read. Talk about opening up ones eyes!

Tony Alessandra Ph.D.
Communicating At Work
  ... and any tape programs he has done thru Nightingale Conant Audio. Dr. Alessandra is not only insightful but one great storyteller and entertaining speaker.

Stephen Covey Ph.D
7 Habits of Highly Effective People
  Absolute necessary material contained here (I still have my first copy from the 80's) BUT one must also read Living The 7 Habits Stories of Courage & Inspiration (the true stories of people who put the 7 Habits to work in their lives)

Upon the Shoulders of Giants

Daniel Goleman Ph.D.
Emotional Intelligence
Social Intelligence
Primal Leadership
> All contain data and the true stories of what it means to be intelligent in many different areas. It's not just about book smarts but, very importantly, people smarts!

Tom Rusk M.D.
The Power of Ethical Persuasion
> Manipulation carries lots of un-wanted baggage & consequences. Persuasion for the better of all should be the goal.

Michael Brooks
Instant Rapport
> The best book I ever read on Neuro Linguistic Programming

Anthony Robbins
Awaken The Giant Within
> Talk about reference points to be motivated-this book has them in abundance.

Ronna Lichtenberg
It's Not Business/ It's Personal : The 9 Relationship Principles That Power Your Career
> I fortunately saw her on a talk show and I ran out and bought her book. Sometimes timing is everything.

8 Keys To Connecting

Keith Harrel
Connect
   And any tape program by him thru Nightingale Conant

Norma Gleason
Proverbs From Around The World
   My seminar on Multi-cultural Communication (sometimes called Diversity Training) is based on the premise we are more alike than different. This book is a foundational truth proving my premise. The world is getting smaller. We must learn to communicate with everyone.

Deborah Tannen Ph.D.
That's Not What I Meant : How Conversational Style Makes or Breaks Relationships
   Good for the soul and your relationships!

Laurie Beth Jones
Jesus CEO
The 4 Elements of Success
   Good information and thought provoking.

Tonya Reiman
The Power of Body Language
   More powerful insight to what people are saying non-verbally.

Upon the Shoulders of Giants

Catherine Blyth
The Art of Conversation
　　It is an art and it is disappearing. Especially her section on How To Listen Actively.

Laura Ingraham
Of Thee I Zing
　　It's a" step back and look see" at what our culture is becoming. A good read because it gives a "look over the shoulder" of what we dare not directly do. Because to stare and then point out the inanity is to risk the label "intolerant". It's a very entertaining thought provoking book.

Malcom Gladwell
Outliers: The Story of Success
　　One perspective, and very entertaining.

Jim Collins
Good To Great
Choose To Be Great
　　Absolute must read for anyone entering or already in the world of business. And don't just read the first one. The second one gives the rest of the story, but don't skip number one.

Jim Rohn
Leading An Inspired Life
　　And any of the many tape programs he did for Nightingale Conant especially the Weekend Seminar with Jim Rohn. Jim recently passed and the world is

much poorer. I put him last but he was one of my earliest mentors. He is at last position because I want to really impress upon you that this man is an essential building block in your quest to be successful. I need not say more.

I am glad you have bought my book. Please keep in mind these *Giants* that allowed me to see further are necessary to speed up your quest to be a success. And success means different things to different people, but there is an essential principle and practice needed regardless of what you define as being successful. This essential is; we need other people and they need us. Fulfilling this need means we must work at communicating so they want to hear and share and help. Just as we wish to hear them, share with them and help them where we can.

Health & Joy to You and Yours!
Darren Murphy

"Truth is ever to be found in the simplicity, and not in the multiplicity and confusion of things."

To know the author of this and the "shoulders of giants" quotes, let the illustrated giant be your clue.
– Darren

CASE STUDIES

CASE STUDIES

CASE STUDY I

You are about to meet that special someone's parents. This one is special because everything seems to click and mesh between the two of you. So you definitely don't want to make a bad first impression.

> "Dad, Mom, this is _____. _____ I'd like you to meet my parents."

You open with ...

> "Mr. and Mrs. ____, I'm glad to meet you."
>
> *– Or –*
>
> It's a pleasure.
>
> *– Or –*
>
> I've been looking forward to meeting you.
>
> *– NOT –*

"Hey"

"Hi"

"What's up"

Even if the parents are gregarious, out-going, and obviously socializer types, you do not act the same 'at this meeting' and not necessarily at the next few meetings. There is an unspoken hierarchy in place. Your place is to defer to their status as parents. And by defer I mean to be focused on them, really pay attention to what they will be asking and saying and be prepared

8 Keys To Connecting

to answer all their questions while simultaneously having questions for them. In fact, while making their questions about you easy for them *(meaning you are eager (55/38/7) to answer)* you too have questions for them *(6 honest serving men)*.

Some topics people like to share about: jobs, childhood hometown, pets, their parents, their hobbies *(look at their environment if you happen to be at their home)*, what's happening in their neighborhood, community or state *(do current topics reading from local paper)*.

Avoid: politics, religion, or any major issue dividing the country. In fact if any subject like that is brought up, some good replies are: *"tell me more"* or *"I haven't kept up. I'm so busy with ..."*, or *"I need to be more informed. Tell me what you have found out."*

* * *

Any further comments or questions?

Visit **www.8keys2connecting.com** *or* **www.8k2c.com** *and let's discuss it.*

CASE STUDIES

CASE STUDY II

You are preparing to have an interview for a job. Whether it is for 'a job' or 'the job' the preparation is the same.

> *I teach interviewing skills and strategies and I always use a sequential approach. The order is essential.*

First prepare to get in the proper mind set. This is accomplished by taking control of your Reticular Activating System *(the filter by which your reality or perception is created)*. And remember you can control your RAS or it can control you.

Taking active control of your RAS for a job interview.

I advise people who take my interview skills and strategies class to specifically think of three questions the owner or the human resource person would want to know. It's more than demographics, or skills, it's much deeper. In order to prepare effectively for these three 'owner type questions' I tell them to put themselves in the mind set of an owner. What would an owner or supervisor want to know? One item definitely: *"Are you a self-starter, proactive?"* Another one might be, *"Are you willing to work overtime?" "Are you willing to research new ways of doing the job?"*

The next three questions you should have prepared are from you as a prospective employee. These are deeper

8 Keys To Connecting

than; how much is the pay, how long is lunch break, where can I smoke, and do I get holiday pay. In fact, other than wages, the others will be answered either in written or verbal form without you asking.

The three questions, and I won't make you work for these because they are easy to assimilate. They're all about you in a very unique way.

> 1. What specifically can I do working for you that will make you very happy you hired me?
>
> 2. If I do these things consistently, will I be rewarded accordingly or is there another level of duties that I can assimilate that will net me higher compensation? For example: I paint well, fast, and the customers like me – all consistently – I get what you've told me. But what if I get other jobs, or get these customers to add on more painting? Can I get a commission, too?
>
> 3. Who is your best employee at present? Can they train me?

Rarely have owners or HR managers heard these type questions. These type questions accomplish two very important things; show you're thinking about their business in relation to your compensation and it's making you very memorable. Their business, your contribution, and you, being the only one who brings these ideas up *(memorable)* ensures you're at the top of the list.

Case Studies

If you are asked what technical know-how you will bring to the job and you do not have any experience in that occupation, then this is a valid reply:

> "I am willing to learn. I will even give free time to learn. I want to be trained by your most capable, knowledgeable employee. And I would like to add: Systems, software, and processes change every 18 to 24 months usually. The people who can learn those systems quickly and use them to effect are people who are good in communication skills. I am good. So I hope to be considered because I know you will be very pleased with me."

In addition to preparing for the interview evaluate for personality style. In this case your 55% should be showing focused attention; sitting up straight and slightly leaning forward. Evaluate for visual, auditory, or kinesthetic words and return in kind. Don't worry about answering questions quickly, in fact repeat the question out loud and preface it with *"do I understand you correctly ..."* And don't think it's foolish to practice interviews ahead of time.

Finally, write the three questions coming from the owner's perspective and your three from your perspective. Write them, say them out loud numerous times and then when it comes time to use, you will come across as polished, poised, and professional.

8 Keys To Connecting

* * *

Any further comments or questions?

Share them at **www.8keys2connecting.com** *or* **www.8k2c.com** *and let's discuss it.*

Supplemental Materials

Supplemental Materials

E-mail Etiquette Tips

Keep in mind: The meaning of your communication is the response you get back.

- *Everyone is Miss, Ms, or Mr. until they tell you otherwise.*

- *Always use 'bcc' (blind carbon copy) when mass mailing. Do not 'cc'(carbon copy) to a group. Someone may not want their e-mail address made common knowledge.*

- *To show emphasis enclose the word or phrase with an asterisk. Do not use upper case letters to spell entire word(s) unless you mean to shout that word.*

- *Spell check – misspellings leave a negative first impression.*

- *Read out loud before sending to check for grammar and syntax.*

- *Acronyms, abbreviations, and emoticons (symbols to express emotions such as ;-) implying a wink) should not be used unless the other party initiates their use. Even then use only the acronyms and abbreviations they have used. Think 3 times before using emoticons: there is a large margin for misinterpretation of your intent.*

- *Snake oil salespeople, rainmakers, and charlatans: do not support them by forwarding chain letters, implied threats, and save-the-child stories.*

- *If you would not put it on your car window, don't write it in an e-mail. Nothing is confidential!*

Voice Mail Etiquette Tips

The Elements Of A Good Voice Mail Greeting

- 1-2 second pause before your greeting is played to callers.

- Your name.

- The name of your organization/department.

- The day of the week.

- What key(s) callers can press on their telephone for immediate assistance.

- When callers can expect a return call.

- The name and extension of a colleague who can provide assistance.

Example:

Hello. This is [name] of the [department name] of Western Kentucky University. For the week of [date] I will be at [where] and not available to answer your call until [date or day]. If you require assistance before then please contact [name of contact] at [telephone number]. If you need to reach someone immediately please dial [dial through number]. Thank you. (19 seconds)

Supplemental Materials

Some Suggested Personal Voice Mail Greetings

Ongoing:

Hello, you have reached the office of [department name]. I am not in my office to take your call. At the tone leave your name, telephone number and details of what I can do for you and I will call you back in the next [time] or so. Thank you.
(17 seconds)

Hi, this is [name] I'm sorry I cannot answer your call right now. Please leave a detailed message at the tone. I'll call you as soon as I return. Thank you.
(15 seconds)

Hello, you have reached the [department name] at Western Kentucky University. I'm sorry I cannot answer your call at the present time. Please leave a message at the tone. I will pass your message onto the appropriate person or call you back. Thank you for calling. Bye.
(17 seconds)

Hello, this is [name] of [department name] at Western Kentucky University. I'm sorry I can't speak with you at the moment, but if you'd like to leave your name, telephone number and details of how I can help you, I'll get back to you as soon as possible. Thank you for calling.
(14 seconds)

8 Keys To Connecting

Daily:

Hello, you have reached the office of [department name] I am interviewing today, Monday, May 2nd, and will not be able to get back to you until after [time]. If you require assistance in the meantime, please call [telephone number]. Thank you.
(16 seconds)

Weekly:

Hello, this is [name]. For the week of [date] I will not be available on Monday morning or Thursday afternoon, but should be in my office the remainder of the week. If you require assistance during my absence, please call [telephone number]. Thank you.
(20 seconds)

Extended Absence:

Hello, you have reached the office of [name]. I am not in today, but will be back in the office on [day of the week] the [date]. Will you please call back then? If you need assistance before then, please call [telephone number]. Thank you.
(15 seconds)

Hello, this is [name]. I'm sorry I am unable to answer your telephone call. I am on leave from [date] until [date] and will not be checking my voice mailbox. If you require assistance in my absence, please contact [telephone number]. Thank you.
(19 seconds)

Supplemental Materials

Hi - [name] - [school name]. I'm sorry I'm not available as I'm overseas until [day and date]. If you have any business which requires my immediate attention, please call [telephone number]. If you have a fax machine available, please send me a fax at [fax number] and I will attend to it as soon as I return. Thanks for your consideration. Cheers now.
(26 seconds)

Extended Absence / Christmas Closedown (or Other Extended) Periods:

Thank you for calling. You have reached [department name]. The University is officially closed over the Christmas-New Year period. I will be back in my office at 8:00 AM, Monday, January __ , 20__. Will you please call back then? Thank you and have a happy holiday season.
(18 seconds)

Forward On Busy:

Hello, this is [name] of [department name]. I'm on another call at the moment, but please don't hang up until you leave your name and your telephone number and I will call you back in [amount of time *(make sure you can meet the time)*] or so. Thank you.
(12 seconds)

Hello, you have reached [name and department]. I'm presently on a call with someone else and I

8 Keys To Connecting

am unable to speak to you personally. However, if you will leave your name and telephone number I will call you back in [time] or so. Thank you.
(13 seconds)

Some ways to help people who call you feel comfortable leaving messages

- *Update your personal greeting regularly.*

- *In your greeting, let callers know when you will return their call.*

- *Include information in your greeting about how callers can reach a colleague who can help them if you are not available.*

- *If you will be away from the office for an extended period, on business or leave, let callers know and tell them how to reach a colleague who is taking your calls.*

- *Tell your callers how they can easily reach someone in real time if their call is urgent. But, make sure an operator or receptionist is available to answer the line during normal business hours.*

- *Pause for 1 - 2 seconds before you record your greetings so that if your mailbox receives a STD call the beginning of your greeting, particularly your name, is not drowned out by the STD pips.*

Suggestions When Considering the Composition of Your Greeting

- *Try keeping your recording to a maximum of about 15 seconds.*

Supplemental Materials

- Do not say "operators are busy" - instead tell callers operators are aware of their call but are attending to others, etc.

- Do not say "you have been placed in a queue" - instead ask callers to hold.

- Wait at least 1-2 seconds before commencing recording your greeting. This gives time for the call to be answered and for the caller to be receptive. Also, it allows the STD pips to be heard and not recorded over.

- Take your time while recording, and sound sincere.

Other Phrases You May Wish to Consider

- Did you know that we ...

- You can also contact us on ...

- If you prefer to fax your inquiry to us, you can do so on ...

- Thank you for calling. One of our reps will be with you shortly.

- Thank you for waiting, we appreciate your patience. One of our reps will (be with) (attend to) you shortly.

Closed and OpenEnded Questions

There are advantages and disadvantages to both types of questions. Understanding these differences assists in knowing when to use which type in order to gather the most informative and accurate information.

8 Keys To Connecting

Closed & Open Ended Questions Characteristics

	CLOSED-ENDED	OPEN-ENDED
DEFINITION	• Yes / No / Short Answer • Forced Choice Response • No Feelings / Emotion / Thinking • Allows for Only One Answer	• Lengthy • With Feeling and Emotion • Often No Single Right Answer
ADVANTAGES	• Creates Fast Pace • Increases Energy • Increases Sense of Urgency	• Creates Critical Thinking • Increases Intellectual Involvement • Increases Self-Esteem
DISADVANTAGES	• Possibly Influence Responses by Forcing or Restricting Choices • Order of Choices Can Affect Results • "Other" and "None of the Above" Is Not Always Informative • Can Fatigue if Overdone	• Requires More Time for Respondents to Give • Difficult to Make Clear-Cut Comparisons • May be More Affected by Interpretation of Person Analyzing Responses
USES	• Good for Data Collection e.g. A Survey	• Good for Relationship Building e.g. One-on-One Time (when using open ended questions with a group use rhetorical ones)

Supplemental Materials

How People Perceive Communication

Generic	Visual	Auditory	Kinesthetic
I understand you.	I see your point	I hear what you are saying.	I feel that I am in touch with what you are saying.
I want to communicate something to you.	I want you to take a look at this.	I want to make this loud and clear.	I want you to get a grasp on this.
Do you understand what I am trying to communicate?	Am I painting a clear picture?	Does what I am saying sound right to you?	Are you able to get a handle on this?
I know that to be true	I know beyond a shadow of a doubt that that is true.	This information is right word for word.	The information is solid as a rock.
I am not sure about that.	That is pretty hazy to me.	That doesn't really ring a bell.	I'm not sure I'm following you.
I don't like what you are doing.	I take a dim view of your perspective	That does not resonate with me at all.	What you're doing doesn't feel right to me.
Life is good.	My mental image of life is sparkling and crystal.	Life is perfect harmony.	Life feels warm and wonderful.

Daily Success Log – Page One

	Success	Reason	Further Progress	Next Action
1				
2				
3				
4				
5				

Supplemental Materials

Daily Success Log – Page Two

	Success	Reason	Further Progress	Next Action
6				
7				
8				
9				
10				

ABOUT THE AUTHOR

While growing up, Darren lived in various locations throughout New England, in California and in Washington, D.C. It was not unusual for him to attend two different school systems in the same year.

Since graduating from high school, he has increased his travels to include Europe, the Middle East, the Philippines and nearly every state in the United States. He has met far more good people in his travels than bad and maintains that has been his experience regardless of whether he is in Turkey, Florida, Belgium, New York, Honduras, California, England, Wyoming, Ireland or the Philippines. In short: there are good people everywhere. He also has encountered toxic people. He warns that toxic people, toxic groups and toxic organizations must be avoided regardless of the benefits they appear to offer.

Darren has been designing and presenting seminars since 1997. Categories covered are all things to do with person-to-person communication. Some of his customized training programs are:

- *Negotiation*
- *Team Building*
- *Manager Skills and Leadership Practices*
- *Avoiding Anger and Conflict*
- *Diversity Training*
- *Neutralizing Workplace Harassment*
- *Memorable Customer Service*
- *Organization Culture.*

Darren Murphy

Each of these seminars has been solicited by private, public and government agencies. You can learn more about them at Darren's seminar training website **www.djmseminars.com**.

Darren, who is also a Registered Nurse, has designed a program specifically to meet the needs of health care facilities titled *Be the Hospital of Choice*. It covers specific issues endemic to health care organizations.

Darren attributes his success to paying attention to all his communication events. Treating these communication exchanges as individual, important and welcomed has provided him with options, opportunities and open doors that previously would never have happened. He shares these skills and strategies in his book, *8 Keys To Connecting*. As an added benefit to increase the power of his book he coaches the individual through to success on his accompanying website, **www.8keys2connecting.com** or **www.8k2c.com** *(if you are into brevity)*.

Darren lives with his wife, Charlotte, in rural Tennessee along with their three horses, two dogs, three cats and nine ducks.

CPSIA information can be obtained at www.ICGtesting.com
Printed in the USA
LVOW050714290612

288018LV00001BA/109/P